JUNIOR BIOGRAPHY FROM

ANCIENT CIVILIZATIONS

SOCRATES

JIM WHITING

Mitchell Lane
PUBLISHERS

P.O. Box 196
Hockessin, Delaware 19707
Visit us on the web: www.mitchelllane.com
Comments? Email us: mitchelllane@mitchelllane.com

JUNIOR BIOGRAPHY FROM ANCIENT CIVILIZATIONS

Alexander the Great • Archimedes
Augustus Caesar • Confucius • Genghis Khan
Homer • Leif Erikson • Marco Polo
Nero • Socrates

ABOUT THE AUTHOR: Jim Whiting has written over 150 nonfiction books for young readers and edited more than 200. His varied career includes publishing *Northwest Runner* magazine, writing hundreds of newspaper and magazine articles, advising an award-winning high school newspaper, and serving as official photographer for the Antarctica Marathon. He lives in Washington state.

PUBLISHER'S NOTE: The facts on which the story in this book is based have been thoroughly researched. Documentation of such research can be found on pages 44–45. While every possible effort has been made to ensure accuracy, the publisher will not assume liability for damages caused by inaccuracies in the data, and makes no warranty on the accuracy of the information contained herein.

Printing 1   2   3   4   5   6   7   8   9

Library of Congress
Cataloging-in-Publication Data

Whiting, Jim, 1943–
  Socrates / by Jim Whiting.
     pages cm. — (Junior biography from ancient civilizations)
  Includes bibliographical references and index.
  ISBN 978-1-61228-433-0 (library bound)
  1. Socrates—Juvenile literature. 2. Philosophers—Greece—Biography—Juvenile literature. I. Title.
  B316.B36 2013
  183'.2—dc23
  [B]

                                    2013012562

eBook ISBN: 9781612284958

                                    PLB

CONTENTS

Phonetic pronunciations of words in **bold**
can be found on page 46.

This statue of the philosopher Socrates is in front of the National Academy in Athens, Greece. The Academy is the country's leading research facility.

CHAPTER 1
On Trial for His Life

One of the most famous trials in world history took place in Athens, Greece, on a spring morning in 399 BCE. The defendant was a man named **Socrates**,* who was 70 years old. Socrates was a famous philosopher. A philosopher is a person who loves wisdom. Because of Socrates's reputation, many people in Athens—especially young men—liked to listen to him so they could learn about philosophy. But not everyone approved of what he had to say. Several Athenian citizens had accused him of some of the most serious crimes in that era and forced him to stand trial.

On this morning, Socrates was on his way to the building where the trial would take place. He met a friend of his, a man named **Euthyphro**. Socrates told him that Meletus, one of his accusers, "has noticed how—in my ignorance—I'm corrupting his contemporaries and goes to the city, as if to his mother, to tell on me."[1] In other words, Socrates was saying that he was supposedly turning young people away from the traditional values of Athens.

*For pronunciations of words in **bold**, see page 46.

Socrates added that Meletus "claims I'm a manufacturer of gods, he says this is why he's prosecuted me, that I create new gods and don't recognize the old ones."[2] This charge was even more serious. Athens worshipped many gods, and it was important that all of them received the respect and homage to which they were entitled. That way they would act favorably toward Athens. Someone who seemed like he was trying to change the form of worship and introduce new gods was dangerous. The traditional gods would be angry. Their anger could be dangerous to the well-being of the city.

So dangerous, in fact, that Socrates's accusers wanted him to suffer the death penalty if he was convicted.

Trials in ancient Athens differed in many ways from how they are conducted today. One of the main differences was the number of jurors. Instead of the six or 12 that are normal today, Athenian juries consisted of 500 men. There were two reasons for having such large juries. One reason was that it was impossible to bribe so many men. The other was that a verdict really represented the will of the people.

The makeup of juries reflected a cross-section of Athenian society. Some of the wealthiest men in Athens were seated next to those with very little money. A prosperous farmer could have a tanner on one side and a stoneworker on the other.

There were no prosecutors or defense attorneys. Accusers spoke directly to the jury, and so did the defendant. Each side had a maximum of three hours to present its case. A slave kept track of the time with a water clock.

Before the trial, each juror received two small bronze discs. Each disc had a tube running through the center. The tube in one disc was hollow, and indicated that the juror believed the defendant was guilty. The other was solid, indicating innocence.

When both sides were done, the jurors formed a line. They filed past two large jars and dropped a disc into the first jar. No one watching could tell which of the two discs they had used. Then they dropped the other disc into the second jar.

Left: Two outflow water clocks from the Museum of the Ancient Agora in Athens. The top is an original from the late 5th century BCE. The bottom is a reconstruction of a clay original.

Right: This water clock pours water for 6 minutes, the allotted time for speech in the law courts in ancient Greece.

When the final man had passed through, the jars were emptied. If there were more "guilty" discs in the first jar, the defendant was convicted. If there were more "not guilty" ones, he was set free. The second jar was just used to verify the results of the first one. Its outcome should be exactly the opposite.

Today, it's common for those who receive guilty verdicts in death penalty cases to spend years and even decades appealing their

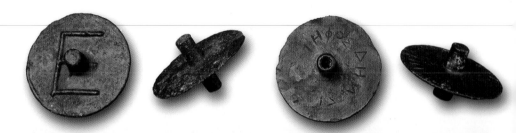

These bronze ballots in the Museum of the Ancient Agora date back to the 4th century BCE. The ballot on the left has a solid axle, indicating innocence in a trial. It is inscribed with an E, representing the Greek letter epsilon. The E might stand for an Athenian tribe. The one on the right has a hollow axle, indicating guilt. It is inscribed "psephos demosia," or public ballot. Most ballots in the museum are made of bronze, with a few made of lead. The majority are from the 4th century BCE, though some are likely to be from the 2nd century BCE.

convictions. In that era, there were no appeals. The sentence was carried out immediately.

So the stakes were high when Socrates arrived at the scene of the trial. It was a square room, nearly 100 feet on each side. Three sides had benches for the jurors and onlookers, and probably some of them sat on the floor. Socrates, his accusers, and the archon (the man who oversaw the trial) sat in chairs on the fourth side.

When everyone was in place, the archon rose to his feet. The trial had begun.

The Gods of Athens

While Athenians worshipped many gods, the most important were the Twelve Olympians, who lived on Mount Olympus.

Zeus was the chief god. He threw thunderbolts at anyone who displeased him. He could change his shape and have affairs with earthly women.

His wife was **Hera**, the goddess of marriage and childbirth.

Poseidon, the sea god, was Zeus's brother. His weapon was a trident, which shook the earth when he was angry.

"The Twelve Olympians" is a drawing by French artist Nicolas-André Monsiau

Hades was another of Zeus's brothers. He was god of the underworld.

Zeus's sister was **Hestia**, goddess of the home. Greek cities had a public hearth devoted to her.

Ares, the god of war, was the son of Zeus and Hera.

Apollo, the god of music and of light, was the son of Zeus and Leto, a mortal woman.

Artemis was Apollo's twin sister. She was goddess of the hunt.

Athena was Zeus's daughter. Born full-grown from Zeus's forehead, she was associated with wisdom.

Hermes was the son of Zeus and Maia, a minor goddess. He was the messenger god.

Hephaestus, the blacksmith god, was the son of Zeus and Hera. While Greek gods were noted for their beauty, Hephaestus was ugly.

His wife was **Aphrodite**, the goddess of love and beauty. Her father was Zeus and her mother was Dione, another minor goddess.

This painting, entitled "Socrates Teaching Perikles," was completed in 1780 by French painter Nicholas Guibal. Perikles (also spelled Pericles) was one of the most important Athenian leaders during the time of

CHAPTER 2
Becoming a Philospher

In his book *A Tale of Two Cities*, famous English novelist Charles Dickens wrote, "It was the best of times, it was the worst of times." Much the same thing is true of the life span of Socrates, who had the good fortune to be born as ancient Athens was about to enter its Golden Age. Yet by the time of his death, Athens was only a shadow of what it had been just a few short years earlier, never to reclaim even a hint of its former greatness.

Most likely Socrates was born in 469 BCE. His father, whose name was **Sophroniscus**, is usually identified as either a sculptor or a stonecutter. **Phaenarete**, his mother, was a midwife.

In that era, Greece consisted of hundreds of city-states. Each city-state was a self-contained political unit, consisting of a central town or city and the surrounding countryside. The population of city-states ranged from a few thousand up to as much as a quarter of a million in Athens, which was perhaps the largest. In general they all spoke Greek and worshiped many of the same gods.

A few decades before Socrates' birth, the city had established what is often considered the world's first democracy. In 490 BCE, an outnumbered Athenian army had soundly defeated the invading Persians at the Battle of Marathon. Ten years later, the Persians returned with one of the largest-ever armies in ancient times. Led by Athens and Sparta, many city-states banded together. They won a stunning naval victory in 480 at Salamis and ended the Persian threat the following year at the Battle of **Plataea**.

Athens soon underwent a flowering of all types of culture. This flowering reached its peak in the span of a few years beginning in 450 under the leadership of **Pericles**, regarded by many historians as Athens' greatest statesman. It was symbolized by the **Parthenon**, a temple dedicated to the goddess Athena and completed in 438. The centerpiece was a massive statue of the deity.

Today, scholars know the detailed history of this era. However, the same thing cannot be said about the life of Socrates. For one thing, he never wrote down anything about himself or his ideas. Almost everything about him comes from several people who knew him. The two most important sources are **Xenophon** and Plato, who were his students. Plato would later write more than 20 dialogues in which Socrates plays the central role. Almost from the day they were written, however, scholars have debated how much of what they say about Socrates is true.

Despite this handicap, however, many events of his life can be dated with some degree of accuracy, especially since so much is known about the customs that existed during this time. According to these customs, five days after his birth his father carried him around the hearth five times to formally have him become a part of the family. Five days after that he received his name.

Athens highly prized literacy, so a number of elementary schools dotted the city. It's almost certain that as the son of a reasonably well-to-do family, Socrates spent several years learning to read and write. He would also have attended a gymnasium, developing a high degree of physical fitness.

When he was eighteen, he officially became an Athenian citizen. That entailed numerous responsibilities, including participation in civic affairs and training with the Athenian army. Athens was a city that loved festivals, chief of which was the **Panathenaea**. Like the Olympic Games, it was held at four-year intervals. According to Plato, Socrates had already begun his interest in philosophy by the year 450. During the Panathenaea that year, he reportedly spent considerable amounts of time talking with Parmenides and Zeno. They were among the era's most famous philosophers.

They weren't the only ones who influenced Socrates. A group of philosophers called Sophists were active in Athens at this time. The "wisdom" they loved often seemed to be their ability to convince other people to accept their line of reasoning. They also taught more general courses, in which it was clear that they believed that their wisdom was greater than their listeners. Most of them, no matter how different their topics or the skills they taught, had one thing in common: they charged money—often lots of money—for their services.

While Socrates frequently encountered the Sophists, there were several important differences between him and them. For one thing, Socrates never charged any more money. It's not clear how he managed to support himself, but somehow he managed to make ends meet.

For another, he never said that he had any particular wisdom to teach. One time a friend of his named **Chaerephon** visited the Oracle of Delphi, a famous ancient shrine that provided answers to important questions. Chaerephon asked the Oracle if anyone was smarter than Socrates. The answer was definitive. There was no one smarter. When Chaerephon happily told Socrates about the response, the philosopher was puzzled. Eventually Socrates concluded that the Oracle was correct. "Everyone else suffered from the false conceit that he knew more than he actually did," says historian Robin Wakefield. "So Socrates concluded that he alone *did* have a kind of wisdom—the sense to know how little he knew."[1] His "smartness" consisted in knowing that he was ignorant about so many things.

Another important difference was that the Sophists often had a common meeting place, where they would conduct their lessons. Not Socrates. His "classroom" was the streets of Athens. He became noted for stopping people at random. He would ask them to state a principle they believed in. Then he would ask questions about that principle. Nearly always, those questions would reveal that the person's reasons for believing in that principle were flawed. Socrates would continue to ask questions, and eventually this process would arrive at an understanding that everyone could agree with.

He explained his process by comparing it to his mother's occupation as a midwife. Because he had no wisdom, he couldn't teach it to others. Instead, he believed that other people had wisdom inside themselves. Like a midwife helping to deliver a baby, his continual questions "gave birth" to a more accurate and realistic belief. This became known as the Socratic Method.

To Socrates, this was the most important thing that he—or anyone else—could do. "'The unexamined life is not worth living for a human being,' as he says at his trial," points out Stanford University philosophy professor Debra Nail. "Socrates pursued this task single-mindedly, questioning people about what matters most, e.g., courage, love, reverence, moderation, and the state of their souls generally. He did this regardless of whether his respondents wanted to be questioned or resisted him; and Athenian youths imitated Socrates' questioning style, much to the annoyance of some of their parents."[2]

Years later, that "annoyance" would take a much more deadly form.

Xenophon and the Ten Thousand

Born in Athens in 430 BCE, Xenophon probably became a student of Socrates by the time he was in his teens. In 401, against Socrates's advice, he joined thousands of other Greek warriors who were enlisted by a Persian prince named Cyrus. Cyrus was trying to claim what he said was his rightful throne and needed an army to help him.

However, Cyrus was killed in battle and the leaders of the Greek warriors were murdered. Known as the Ten Thousand, the warriors were stranded hundreds of miles from home. They elected Xenophon as one of their leaders.

Bernard Granville Baker's 1901 painting "The Sea! "The Sea!" reflects the joy of the Ten Thousand at the end of their journey.

After many battles and adventures during the next two years, they finally reached safety. About 6,000 of the original number survived. Xenophon eventually retired to southern Greece, where he spent most of the rest of his life writing about his experiences—which included his time with Socrates.

In 1979, a film called *The Warriors* used the Ten Thousand as its inspiration. A New York City gang called the Warriors joins a summit meeting of all the city's gangs. The man who organized the meeting is murdered and the Warriors are falsely accused of killing him. They have to make their way home through a series of hostile environments.

A portrait of Socrates as a young man. It may reflect his appearance at the beginning of his career as one

CHAPTER 3
Socrates as a Soldier

But even as Socrates was becoming better known in Athens and attracting an increasingly larger number of followers, events far beyond his control were tearing at the very structure of Athenian society.

In World War II, the United States and the Soviet Union became allies against Germany even though their political and social systems were very different. As soon as the war was over, they became bitter enemies. While they never fought an actual war against each other, the tensions led to much global uncertainty and anxiety until the Soviet Union collapsed in 1990.

Something similar happened in Greece. The differences between Sparta and Athens created tensions soon after they had combined to defeat the Persians. The two sides and their allies fought several battles between 460 and 445, though they finally agreed on a truce.

It didn't last very long. In 432 Athens attacked the city-state of **Potidaea**, which had revolted against Athenian control. Both Socrates and

Alcibiades, a rising young nobleman who was still in his teens, were part of the Athenian force which won an initial battle and then settled in for a long siege. The bulk of the fighting was done by heavily armed men known as hoplites. They wore bronze armor that covered much of their bodies and heads, and carried long spears and heavy shields. Hoplites were expected to furnish their own equipment. Because all evidence indicates that Socrates was a hoplite, somehow he could afford it even though he didn't take any money for his teaching.

Sometime during this campaign Socrates came to Alcibiades's rescue in a dangerous situation. "I will also tell, if you please—and

French artist François-André Vincent completed this work, "Alcibiades Being Taught by Socrates," in 1777. Alcibiades became one of the most important Athenian leaders late in the 5th century BCE and Socrates had a significant influence on his development.

Greece, 431 B.C.

Cities
- • neutral
- • Sparta & allies
- • Athens & allies

0   50   100   200 Kilometers

This map of Greece at the start of the Peloponnesian War in 431 BCE shows the location of the two primary combatants, Athens and Sparta, as well as the city-states that aligned themselves with each of them.

indeed I am bound to tell—of his [Socrates'] courage in battle; for who but he saved my life?" Alcibiades told the guests at a party both he and Socrates were attending years later. "I was wounded and he would not leave me, but he rescued me and my arms."[1]

Beyond the battlefield at Potidaea, there were two major developments. One was the outbreak of the **Peloponnesian** War in 431. It was basically a civil war pitting Sparta and its allies against Athens and its allies, and would eventually transform the entire Greek landscape. The second was the outbreak of a deadly plague in Athens the following year. The disease claimed thousands of lives, including Pericles and many of the city's leading citizens. Many survivors

French artist Jean-Léon Gérôme painted "Socrates Seeking Alcibiades in the House of Aspasia" in 1861. Aspasia was one of the most famous hostesses in Athens. Many of the city's most powerful men attended her parties.

believed that it was a punishment from the gods for neglecting them. Some of the city's famous freedom of expression disappeared.

Socrates was among the survivors, and—often to the dismay of his friends, many of whom stayed cooped up inside their homes to lessen the chances of becoming infected—continued his usual practice of walking the streets and talking to anyone who would listen to him.

Socrates was called to military service again in 424. The Athenians attacked the city-state of Delium. At first the battle went well for the Athenians, but as it progressed their forces were pushed back and many men panicked. Socrates didn't. Laches, an Athenian general, said that Socrates "was my companion in the retreat from Delium, and I can tell you that if others had only been like him, the honour of our country would have been upheld, and the great defeat would never have occurred."[2]

Alcibiades also praised Socrates. "He [Socrates] and Laches were retreating, for the troops were in flight, and I met them and told them not to be discouraged, and promised to remain with them; and there you might see him," he said, "just as he is in the streets of Athens, stalking like a pelican, and rolling his eyes, calmly contemplating enemies as well as friends, and making very intelligible to anybody, even from a distance, that whoever attacked him would be likely to meet with a stout resistance; and in this way he and his companion escaped—for this is the sort of man who is never touched in war; those only are pursued who are running away headlong. I particularly observed how superior he was to Laches in presence of mind."[3]

Two years later, Socrates went to war for the third time as the Athenians tried to recapture the city of **Amphipolis**, which the Spartans had taken in 424. Unlike the other two campaigns, there are no reports about his actions—perhaps because the disorganized Athenians were routed and lost more than 600 men to just eight for the Spartans. The survivors returned to Athens. Socrates would never leave the city again.

Hoplite Warfare

In Socrates' era, hoplite warfare was very common. The word "hoplite" comes from the Greek word *hoplon*, which refers to the large circular shields the men carried for protection. They also wore heavy bronze armor. Their primary weapons were long spears and swords.

Before the battle began, the hoplites would arrange themselves in what is known as a **phalanx**, consisting of about eight or ten rows of heavily armed men. They were packed very tightly together, because each man carried his shield on his left arm. That left part of his right side unprotected, though the man to his right covered that area.

Greek phalanx

At a signal, both sides would advance toward each other, their spears protruding out in front of their massed shields. When they collided, the men in the back rows would push forward, trying to create enough pressure to push the other side backward. As men in the front rows began to suffer spear wounds and fall, the ones behind them would take their place.

Finally one side would break and the men would turn and flee. At that point the hoplites on the victorious side would pull out their swords and try to kill their disheartened enemies.

Socrates and his wife Xanthippe had a relationship that was often stormy. Italian artist Luca Giordano (1634–1705) captures one of their conflicts in his painting "Xanthippe Pouring Water onto Socrates' Neck."

CHAPTER 4
Dark Days for Athens

Many scholars believe that soon after the Battle of Amphipolis, Socrates finally got married, to a woman named **Xanthippe**. Soon afterward they had a son. They named him **Lamprocles**, perhaps after Xantippe's father. Her father would have provided a dowry, helping Socrates and his new family meet the costs of daily life. Later the couple would have two more sons, Sophroniscus (after Socrates' father) and **Menexenos**.

Apparently Socrates and his wife didn't get along well. "In one episode that has given great delight to cartoonists and engravers down the centuries, Xanthippe, raging after one argument with her maddening philosopher spouse, pours the contents of a bedpan over Socrates' head; 'I always knew that rain would follow thunder,' sighs the philosopher, resignedly mopping his brow."[1]

Perhaps there was another source of friction between them. At the time of the marriage, Socrates was probably in his late 40s, while Xanthippe would probably have been a teenager or in her early 20s. Athens was a city in which physical attractiveness was very important and played a key role in political and social advancement. Greek statues from this era all emphasize the beauty of their subjects. Yet Socrates didn't fit this mold. As Stanford philosophy professor Debra Nails says, "The extant sources agree that Socrates was profoundly ugly. . . . He had wide-set, bulging eyes that darted sideways and enabled him, like a crab, to see not only what was straight ahead, but what was beside him as well; a flat, upturned nose with flaring nostrils; and large fleshy lips like an ass. Socrates let his hair grow long, Spartan-style (even while Athens and Sparta were at war), and went about barefoot and unwashed, carrying a stick and looking arrogant. He didn't change his clothes but efficiently wore in the daytime what he covered himself with at night."[2]

Outside of the city, things grew progressively worse. Alcibiades had steadily risen in importance in Athens. In 415 he urged an attack on the Greek colony of **Syracuse**, located on the island of Sicily. The attack was a total disaster and Alcibiades was widely blamed for the defeat. He fled to Sparta, where he advised the Spartans against Athens.

Gradually Sparta gained the upper hand in the Peloponnesian War. Athens gained a brief respite in 406, when its fleet defeated the Spartans in the Battle of **Arginusae**. But a severe storm prevented the victorious generals from retrieving the corpses of their dead, which was a violation of Athenian law. Nor could they retrieve the survivors of sunken ships, many of whom drowned. When they returned to the city, they were placed on trial—as a group. This was also a violation of Athenian law, which insisted on trying people as individuals. That didn't matter to the thousands of the generals' fellow citizens, who wanted to charge them with anti-democratic activity.

By chance, Socrates was the presiding officer of the court that day. He spoke out against trying the generals as a group because it violated the law. It had long been known that in spite of his popularity, Socrates was not in favor of democracy. But he was in favor of following the

Alcibiades abandoned Athens during the Peloponnesian War and helped the Spartans for several years. He had a change of heart and returned to Athens in 407 BCE. Surprisingly, the citizens welcomed him back with open arms and he helped them win several battles.

law. When people in the crowd shouted at him that he was committing treason, he responded that he was only doing what was legal. Finally darkness fell. The following day brought a new presiding officer, who went along with the crowd's demands. The generals were quickly found guilty and executed.

Two years later Athens finally surrendered and the war ended. Almost immediately a group of men known as The Thirty took

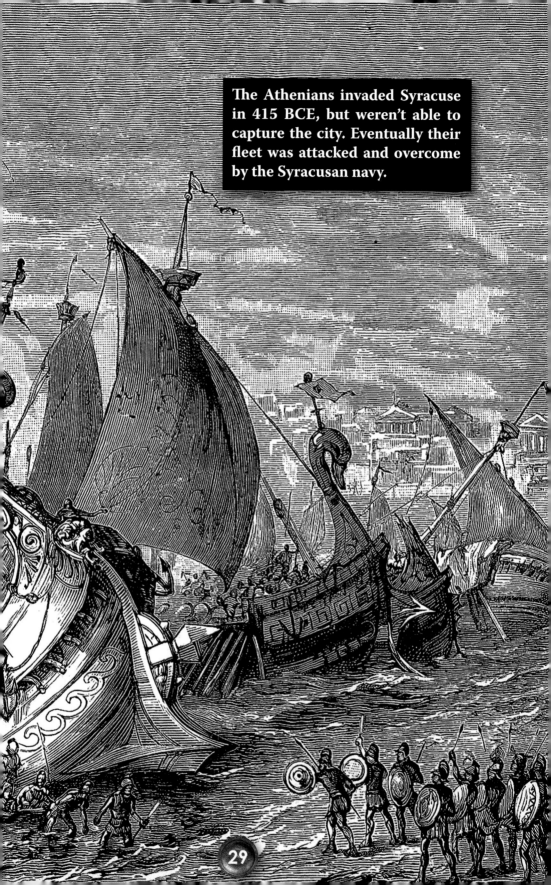

The Athenians invaded Syracuse in 415 BCE, but weren't able to capture the city. Eventually their fleet was attacked and overcome by the Syracusan navy.

Alcibiades made many enemies during the Peloponnesian War because he kept switching sides. He tried to find shelter in Phrygia (in modern-day Turkey) in the war's final days, but he was tracked down and killed in 404 BCE. He was about 45 at the time.

control of the city. Under the leadership of Critias, one of Socrates' former students, they ordered more than 1,500 men to be executed.

One victim was Leon of Salamis. Socrates and four other men were ordered to arrest him. As Socrates later explained, "They gave many such orders to others also, because they wished to implicate as many in their crimes as they could."[3]

Though the other four men obeyed the order, Socrates refused. This refusal could have harmed him. The Thirty didn't like anyone who wouldn't go along with them. Fortunately for Socrates, they were overthrown soon afterward and the democracy was restored.

Socrates had escaped the vengeance of The Thirty, but now he faced a new form of anger. Many people were unhappy with The Thirty and anyone associated with them. Their thirst for vengeance was deep. Socrates was directly in the crosshairs.

Syracuse

Syracuse, which had been founded many years earlier, was an ally of Sparta. Alcibiades urged an attack on the city in 415, but he was recalled to Athens while the invading fleet was en route to Syracuse.

While the Athenian forces nearly captured the city within a short time, a Spartan general named **Gylippus** rallied the Syracusans and prevented its takeover. The Athenians sent reinforcements but their commanders disagreed among themselves and didn't take advantage of an opportunity that would probably have given them a victory.

Soon they found themselves surrounded by enemy forces. A chain stretched across the harbor entrance kept them from escaping by sea. In 413, a final desperate attempt to escape overland failed. Most of the remaining Athenians were sent to the stone quarries and worked to death. A few managed to escape and brought news of the defeat to Athens.

The final defeat of the Athenian navy in the Great Harbor of Syracuse in 413 BCE.

It's likely that the city lost 200 ships and more than 10,000 men. Historians generally regard the defeat as the turning point in the war, and many express surprise that the depleted Athenian forces were able to continue the war for nearly 10 more years.

Russian sculptor Mark Antokolski created "The Death of Socrates" in 1875. Today it is in the Russian Museum in St. Petersburg.

Today, it's hard to determine what actually happened at Socrates' trial. There is no record of what Socrates' accusers said. But his admirers, especially Plato and Xenophon, offered lengthy narratives of how he tried to defend himself.

One thing seems undeniable. Socrates strongly disapproved of democracy. As the past few years had demonstrated, the entire system of Athenian democracy was shaky. Its supporters may have viewed Socrates as a danger. And in a society that was so religiously oriented, their recent struggles—especially the defeat in the Peloponnesian War—could be taken as a sign of divine displeasure. So the charge of impiety was not one to be taken lightly.

Socrates often described himself as a gadfly, pestering people in his efforts to make them examine their lives. But in one of the dialogues that Plato later wrote, a man named Meno says that Socrates was like a stingray, delivering a shock that temporarily numbs the victim. It's likely that Socrates had done a "full stingray" on

Socrates defends himself during his trial. This scene shows just a handful of the 500 jurors who decided his fate. The Parthenon, Athens' most famous temple, is atop the hill in the background.

at least a few of the jurors. Some of them may have seen a chance to get back at their one-time tormentor.

If they did have resentment toward Socrates and wanted him to humble himself by begging for mercy, they were disappointed. "It is my belief that no greater good has ever befallen you in this city than my service," he said. "Whether you acquit me or not, you know that I am not going to alter my conduct."[1]

When both sides had had their say, the jurors dropped their ballots into the two jars. By a vote of 280 to 220, Socrates was found guilty.

The next step was deciding on the punishment. Those convicted of crimes carrying the death penalty could propose a lesser sentence, such as temporary exile. Historians believe that many jurors who voted to convict Socrates thought he would choose this option.

But at his age, "temporary exile" almost certainly meant that he would never return to Athens. As historian Paul Johnson notes, "His love of Athens was boundless, and the value he attached to the privilege of being free to walk its streets and talk and argue with its people was the spring of his life and all its motions. He could not be without it, and therefore never considered exile. Athens to Socrates was life."[2]

Rather than proposing exile, Socrates said that his "punishment" should be free meals for the rest of his life. This was one of the highest honors an Athenian could achieve, such as winning an event at the Olympic Games.

Enraged at his flip tone, nearly 100 of his former supporters joined the others in demanding the death penalty. Socrates' fate was sealed. He was taken to a nearby jail to await execution.

The Greek gods seemed to favor Socrates. Customarily a sentence would be carried out within 24 hours of the verdict. But under Athenian law, no executions could occur during the annual Delia festival. The festival honored the Greek god Apollo and took place on the island of Delos. The official Athenian ship had set sail the day

Socrates is seen reaching for the cup of hemlock which will end his life in French painter Jean-François Pierre Peyron's 1787 work, "The Death of Socrates." According to most reports, Socrates was composed and willingly faced his death.

before the trial. When the festival ended, the wind blew in the wrong direction for an extended period of time and the ship had to stay at Delos. Finally the wind shifted enough and the vessel returned, officially ending the festival—and Socrates's reprieve.

Now it was time. The jailer came in with a cup of poison hemlock. To save money, the friends and family of the condemned person had to pay for the hemlock. In a way, Socrates was lucky. This form of execution had only been introduced a few years earlier and still wasn't in common use. Before that Athenians used a type of crucifixion.

The effects began almost immediately and started with feelings of numbness in the legs. Soon Socrates's entire body was paralyzed. Death came as a result of asphyxiation because he could no longer draw air into his lungs.

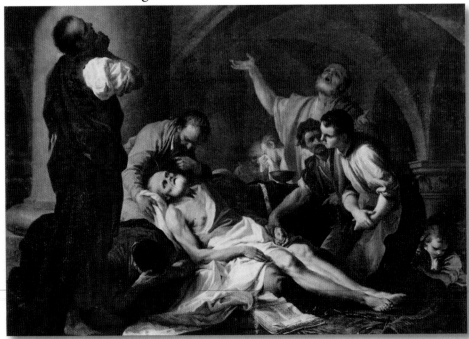

Italian painter Giambettino Cignaroli (1706–1770) depicts another version of Socrates' execution in "The Death of Socrates."

Socrates' life was over. His legend was about to begin. His student Plato would make him immortal.

Plato and the Perfect Government

Even before the trial of Socrates, Plato held a very low opinion of democracy. He didn't think that most people were smart enough to govern themselves. He was furious that the democratic government of Athens had convicted Socrates and executed him. So he devoted much of his later writings to what he thought was the ideal political system.

At the bottom were the mass of people, who were expected only to do their jobs—such as producing food and providing useful services. They couldn't be allowed to enjoy art, music, and poetry because those would distract them. Men who were especially courageous and aggressive would become soldiers and protect the society.

At the very top were the philosopher-kings, who would be identified at a young age and then undergo long years of training and a variety of types of education. By the age of 50, Plato believed, they would finally be ready to take on the task for which they had been preparing almost their entire lives: ruling the state in a manner which would benefit everyone. As historian Thomas Cahill notes, these philosopher-kings "have been strictly educated to know always what is right and just for themselves and for others. Knowing what is right, they will always choose what is right."[3]

German painter Anselm Feuerbach depicts Socrates and other Athenian thinkers in "Plato's Symposium," an 1873 work.

All dates Before Common Era (BCE)

469	Socrates is born in Athens to Sophroniscus, a stone mason and sculptor, and Phainrete, a midwife.
ca. 460	Socrates begins his formal education.
451	Socrates becomes a citizen.
450	He meets the philosophers Zeno and Parmenides
ca. 440	Socrates begins using the Socratic Method when he meets his fellow citizens.
432-429	Socrates is part of the Athenian army that attacks and then besieges Potidaea; he saves Alcibiades' life.
424	Socrates fights heroically in the Battle of Delium.
423	The comic play, *Clouds*, which makes fun of Socrates, is first performed.
422	Socrates takes part in the Battle of Amphipolis.
ca. 420	Socrates marries Xanthippe.
406	Though Athenian law required that a group of generals had to be tried as individuals, the citizens wanted to try them together. Socrates refused to go along with this plan.
404	Socrates defies The Thirty tyrants.
399	Socrates dies from drinking poison hemlock after being convicted of impiety and of corrupting the youth of Athens.

Sculpture of
Socrates in
the Louvre
Museum in
Paris, France

All dates Before Common Era (BCE)

ca. 1200	The Greeks fight Troy in the Trojan War.
776	The first Olympic Games are held at Olympia, Greece.
ca. 700	Homer writes epic poems *The Iliad* and *The Odyssey*.
509	In Athens, male citizens are allowed to vote on how the city is run. Women and non-citizens are not allowed to vote.
490	A Persian army of more than 20,000 men is defeated by 10,000 Athenians in the Battle of Marathon.
479	The Greeks defeat the Persian Army at the Battle of Plataea.
447	Pericles begins building the Parthenon as a symbol of the "Golden Age" of Athens; it is completed nine years later.
430	The city of Athens is devastated by a plague.
429	Pericles dies from the plague.
404	Athens surrenders to Sparta and The Thirty take over the government.
403	Democracy is restored in Athens.
387	Plato opens the Academy in Athens.
380	Plato finishes writing *The Republic*.
335	Plato's student Aristotle founds the Lyceum in Athens.
322	Aristotle dies.

Chapter 1—On Trial
1. Plato, *The Last Days of Socrates*, translated by Hugh Tredennick and Harold Tarrant (New York: Penguin Books, 2003), pp. 9–10.
2. Ibid., p. 10.

Chapter 2—Becoming a Philosopher
1. Robin Wakefield, *Why Socrates Died: Dispelling the Myths* (New York: W.W. Norton, 2009), p. 10.
2. Debra Nails, "Socrates," *The Stanford Encyclopedia of Philosophy* (Spring 2010 Edition), Edward N. Zalta (editor). http://plato.stanford.edu/archives/spr2010/entries/socrates/

Chapter 3—Socrates the Soldier
1. Plato, *Symposium*, translated by Benjamin Jowett. Project Gutenberg, 2008.
   http://www.gutenberg.org/files/1600/1600-h/1600-h.htm
2. Plato, *Laches*, translated by Benjamin Jowett. Project Gutenberg, 2008. http://www.gutenberg.org/files/1584/1584-h/1584-h.htm
3. Plato, *Symposium*.

Chapter 4—Dark Days for Athens
1. Bettany Hughes, *The Hemlock Cup: Socrates, Athens and the Search for the Good Life* (New York: Vintage Books, 2012), p. 155.
2. Debra Nails, "Socrates," *The Stanford Encyclopedia of Philosophy* (Spring 2010 Edition), Edward N. Zalta (editor). http://plato.stanford.edu/archives/spr2010/entries/socrates/
3. I.F. Stone, *The Trial of Socrates* (New York: Anchor Books, 1989), p. 113.

Chapter 5—Guilty as Charged
1. Plato, *The Last Days of Socrates*, translated by Hugh Tredennick and Harold Tarrant (New York: Penguin Books, 2003), p. 56.
2. Paul Johnson, *Socrates: A Man for Our Times* (New York: Viking, 2011), p. 156.
3. Thomas Cahill, *Sailing the Wine-Dark Sea: Why the Greeks Matter* (New York: Anchor Books, 2003), p. 183.

Books

Bordessa, Kris. *Tools of the Ancient Greeks*. White River Junction, VT: Nomad Press, 2006.

Bowen, Richard. *Socrates: Greek Philosopher* (Great Names). Broomall, PA: Mason Crest, 2002.

Dell, Pamela. *Socrates: Ancient Greek in Search of Truth*. Minneapolis, MN: Compass Point Books, 2006.

Lim, Jun. *Socrates: The Public Conscience of Golden Age Athens* (The Library of Greek Philosophers). New York: Rosen, 2006

Usher, M.D. *Wise Guy: The Life and Philosophy of Socrates*. New York: Farrar Giroux & Strauss, 2005.

Van Vleet, Carmella. *Explore Ancient Greece*. White River Junction, Vermont: Nomad Press, 2008.

Zannos, Susan. *The Life and Times of Socrates*. Hockessin, DE: Mitchell Lane Publishers, 2005.

Works Consulted

Cahill, Thomas. *Sailing the Wine-Dark Sea: Why the Greeks Matter*. New York: Anchor Books, 2004.

Guthrie, William Keith Chambers. *Socrates*. Cambridge, United Kingdom: Cambridge University Press, 1971.

Hughes, Bettany. *The Hemlock Cup: Socrates, Athens, and the Search for the Good Life*. New York: Vintage Books, 2012.

Johnson, Paul. *Socrates: A Man for Our Times*. New York: Viking, 2011.

Stone, I.F. *The Trial of Socrates*. New York: Anchor Books, 1989.

Waterfield, Robin. *Why Socrates Died: Dispelling the Myths*. New York: W.W. Norton, 2009.

On the Internet

Linder, Doug. The Trial of Socrates.
http://law2.umkc.edu/faculty/projects/ftrials/socrates/socratesaccount.html

Nails, Debra. "Socrates," The Stanford Encyclopedia of Philosophy (Spring 2010 Edition), Edward N. Zalta (editor).
http://plato.stanford.edu/archives/spr2010/entries/socrates/

Plato, *Laches*, translated by Benjamin Jowett. Project Gutenberg, 2008.
http://www.gutenberg.org/files/1584/1584-h/1584-h.htm

Plato, *Symposium*, translated by Benjamin Jowett. Project Gutenberg, 2008.
http://www.gutenberg.org/files/1600/1600-h/1600-h.htm

Statues of the ancient Greek philosophers Plato (left) and Socrates (right) flank the entrance of the Academy of Athens in Greece.

Alcibiades
(al-kuh-BYE-uh-deez)

Amphipolis
(am-FEE-puh-luhss)

Aphrodite (aa-froh-DIE-tee)

Apollo (uh-PAWL-loh)

Arginusae (ahr-juh-NOO-sigh)

Artemis (AHR-tehm-iss)

Athena (uh-THEE-nuh)

Chaerephon (CARE-uh-fawn)

Euthyphro (YOU-thuh-fro)

Gylippus (JY-luh-pus)

Hades (HAY-deez)

Hephaestus (huh-FACE-tuss)

Hera (HERE-uh)

Hermes (HER-meez)

Hestia (HES-tee-uh)

Lamprocles
(LAAM-proe-cleez)

Menexenos
(muh-NEX-uh-nohss)

Panathenaea
(pan-uh-THEEN-ee-uh)

Parthenon (PAR-thuh-nahn)

Peloponnesian
(pehl-oh-poe-NEE-zhuhn)

Pericles (PAIR-uh-cleez)

Phaenarete (feh-nuh-REE-tee)

phalanx (fuh-LANKS)

Plataea (pluh-TEE-uh)

Poseidon (POE-sye-duhn)

Potidaea (poe-toe-DAY-uh)

Socrates (SAWK-ruh-teez)

Sophroniscus
(sawf-roe-NISS-kuss)

Syracuse (SEAR-uh-cuze)

Xantippe (zan-THIH-pee)

Xenophon (ZEHN-oh-fon)

Zeus (ZOOS)

bedpan (BED-pan)—Receptacle for urine and feces.

bribe (BRYB)—Payment of money or favors to a person to influence their judgment.

conceit (cuhn-SEET)—Belief.

deity (DEE-uh-tee)—Divine being, usually a god or goddess.

dowry (DOW-ree)—Money or property a wife brings to her husband when they are married.

exile (EK-sile)—Banishment from one's native land.

homage (AWM-uhj)—Honor or respect displayed publicly.

midwife (MIHD-wyf)—Person, usually a woman, who assists in childbirth.

quarries (KWOR-eez)—Pits from which stone or other materials are taken.

reprieve (ree-PREEV)—Postponement or cancellation of a punishment.

spouse (SPOUSS)—Married person.

tanner (TAN-nehr)—Person employed to tan animal hides.

treason (TREE-zuhn)—Crime of betraying one's country.

trident (TRY-duhnt)—Spear with three points at the tip.

water clock (WAH-tuhr CLAWK)—Clock that uses the flow of water to tell time.

PHOTO CREDITS: Cover, p. 1—Jacques-Louis David; pp. 4, 16, 34, 45—Photos.com; p. 7—Marsyas/cc-by-sa/2.5; pp. 8, 23, 30, 31, 41—Library of Congress; p. 9—Monsiau p. 10—Nicolas Guibal; p. 15—Bernard Granville Baker; p. 18—François André Vincent; p. 19—Abu America/cc-by-sa/2.5; pp. 20–21—Jean-Léon Gérôme; p. 24—DEA/L. Pedicini/Getty Images; p. 27—Kean Collection/Getty Images; pp. 28–29—Time Life Pictures/Mansell/Getty Images; p. 32—Mark Antokolski; pp. 36–37—Jean François Pierre Peyron; p. 38—Giambettino Cignaroli; p. 39—Anselm Feuerbach. Every effort has been made to locate all copyright holders of materials used in this book. Any errors or omissions will be corrected in future editions of the book.